The Power of Perseverance

By

Natalya H. Bah, PMP, MSPM

and

Carl F. Hicks, Jr., Ph.D.

Copyright © 2020 by Natalya H. Bah
and Carl F. Hicks, Jr.
All rights reserved.

This book or any portion thereof may not be
reproduced or used in any manner whatsoever
without the express written permission of the author.
An exception will be made for reviewers, who
may quote short excerpts from this work
in a review.

ISBN-13: 978-1727594508

High Impact Publishing, Chevy Chase, Maryland
www.HighImpactPublishing.com

Printed in the United States of America

The Power of Perseverance

Table of Contents

Introduction 9

1. Change and Perseverance 15

2. Measuring Your Perseverance 23

3. Optimizing Perseverance 35

Conclusion 45

About the Authors 52

Excerpts from the Power Series 67

    The Power of Perspective Excerpt 69
    The Power of Purpose Excerpt 77
    The Power of Passion Excerpt 85
    The Power of Preparation Excerpt 91
    The Power of Positivity Excerpt 99

A Note from the Authors

Successful individuals in all walks of life often exhibit similar patterns of thinking and behaving. The authors believe it is helpful for those of you on a success journey to have the opportunity to read about and reflect upon these successful patterns of thinking and behaving that we have observed.

The authors have identified the Success Mindsets as Perspective, Purpose, and Passion and the Success Accelerators as Preparation, Positivity, and Perseverance. Each concise book in the series gives an overview of the topic identified. Additionally, each book provides questions to help you consider and increase your own level of these mindsets and accelerators.

Introduction

"On the steep slope of success can be found the victorious who are determined to persevere and to reach their dream."

–Carl Hicks,
Co-Author

After eighteen years of trying, Sergio Garcia won the Masters on Sunday, April 9, 2017 in his 74th attempt at winning a major golf title. He began his journey in 1999 when he first captivated golf fans at the PGA Championship. Over the years, he encountered one disappointment after another with losses and close wins. Garcia persevered through hardships and frustration and teaches us all to never give up. He's a true champion, not just because he won, but because he never gave up on his dream.

Success stories have three major parts: the beginning, middle and end. In measuring success, we often focus on the difference between the start of our success journey and the completion or results achieved. The middle part, the route between start and finish, can contain ups and downs, starts and stops, and zigs and zags. It's rarely a straight line. The middle part of success can be a mixed bag.

It's in this middle part when you may start to experience obstacles. Situations can become complex and people frustrating. Sometimes, it may seem that the harder you work the further behind you get, or you may feel trapped by circumstances beyond your control. Negative emotions can start to dominate your thinking and affect your behavior. You may entertain the idea of quitting. It is precisely at this time that you will need to dig deep inside of yourself and pull up all of your perseverance reserves.

We like to define perseverance as the ability to steadfastly stay the course in the pursuit of a goal, task, dream or journey regardless of the difficulties, distractions or obstacles faced or the frustration and discouragement experienced. What do you think of when you hear the word perseverance? When was the last time to considered how your ability to persevere impacts your life?

The Brick Walls

"The brick walls are there for a reason. The brick walls are not there to keep us out. The brick walls are there to give us a chance to show how badly we want something."

-Randy Pausch,

Author, **The Last Lecture**

Throughout life we are faced with adversity, disappointments, defeats, setbacks, and frustration. Sometimes these "brick walls" can be avoided, and sometimes they cannot.

The question is, how will we respond to the "brick wall"? How will we label the adversity? Will we see it as a disaster that we cannot rise above, or as an opportunity to learn and keep moving?

The choice is ours.

We can choose to stop and give up, saying, "the price is too high, the difficulty too great." Or, we can say, "What can I do now to get where I want to go and to be what I want to be?"

The brick walls can halt us. Or, we can choose to go over or around them. It all depends on "how badly you want something."

Chapter One

Change and Perseverance

"Change is hard at first, messy in the middle and gorgeous at the end."

- Robin Sharma,
Author, Motivational Speaker

In a success journey, much of your growth experience comes from experiencing life along the journey rather than reaching a specific destination. You can become stronger as a person—which in itself is a success trait—by encountering and overcoming roadblocks, potholes, and detours. Perseverance—the drive to continue despite the obstacles—is the success accelerator that will help you reach your destination and grow from your experiences.

When it comes to pursuing and achieving your goals, it is not always convenient, easy, or pleasant. You may struggle. It may take you longer than you thought and be more difficult than you imagined. This is especially true when you may have to develop new skills, create new methods of doing things, or adjust your thinking to incorporate new or different concepts. In short, you will probably have to change, and change is not always easy, convenient, or pleasant.

Real growth always requires change.

In your greatness journey, not only will you have to overcome external obstacles, you will also have to contend with "internal" obstacles. Since personal change involves thinking differently, doing things differently, or becoming different in some way, it usually pushes us out of our comfort zone. And it's not easy. For example, changing your way of thinking about a particular person or situation is difficult for most.

First, we have to realize we need to change in the first place. Once we realize we need to change, we may need to adopt a new perspective about people or situations. Abraham Lincoln said, "I don't much like that man. Perhaps I should get to know him better." This statement alone will not make a difference in a person's relationship with another, but it is a good, first start.

To realize change, you'll have to overcome unproductive habits and "stinkin' thinkin'." Obstacles, such as inertia, ego, habit, and contentment, lay in wait to derail your efforts. However, once you change your thinking, it changes your behavior. And once you change your behavior, the things you want to have happen begin happening.

Personal growth involves letting go of the old and embracing the new.

Your willingness to change is a choice you get to make. By nature, some people are reluctant to embrace change, especially when imposed by others or by outside circumstances. Other people love to introduce change to others, but they may be somewhat reluctant to change themselves. And some people love change. They thrive on it and crave the novelty and variety. In any event, perseverance can be a key skill to ensuring that you see change through.

> **How do you feel about change?**

Don't Get Stuck In Reverse

"Don't dwell on what went wrong. Instead, focus on what to do next. Spend your energies on moving forward toward finding the answer."

- Denis Waitley,
American Motivational Speaker, Writer, Consultant

On any given day we may feel that things are not going well for us. We have too many uncontrollable demands on our time and resources. We feel overwhelmed. This often leads to us not getting tasks done and to frustration, the feeling that we are being blocked from achieving our goals.

Being overwhelmed and frustrated is like trying to rewind your movie and continuing to miss the place you are trying to stop it. Sometimes you need to just hit pause and take a moment to focus. You can use a pause to clarify the tasks or initiatives you want to accomplish or prioritize your "to do" list.

Now, press the play button. You're moving forward once again and able to accomplish your initiatives.

When things are moving, growing, flourishing, you've hit the fast-forward button, the feelings of being overwhelmed and frustrated are far behind you. You are in your zone and in control of your life!

Chapter Two

Measuring Your Perseverance

"I have never had to face anything that could overwhelm the native optimism and stubborn perseverance I was blessed with."

—Sonia Sotomoyer,
United States Supreme Court Justice

Carl once worked in an organization which functioned well based on procedures, processes, and protocols. The organization attracted people who were process oriented and comfortable dealing with known and effective repetitive situations. While Carl was successful in his initial role, he was not fulfilled. His strengths reside in visualizing opportunities, creating ways of accomplishing results, and anticipating and avoiding issues that could become problems. The initial role he had didn't fully realize his strengths.

Leadership recognized this and allowed Carl to rewrite his job description every year for three consecutive years. They encouraged him to introduce new ways to think about old problems, new processes to address existing work flows, and "crazy" concepts to stimulate thinking.

Eventually, Carl outgrew the arrangement. His goals for himself and for his work contributions had increased, and he needed a larger canvas to paint on. With the blessings of leadership, he struck out on his own and transformed a part-time consulting hobby into a full-time business. For his dream of pursuing fulfillment, he left secure employment and gave up a regular paycheck, promotions, and raises.

After leaving the organization and starting his own business, Carl had coffee with a former colleague. He said he didn't understand how Carl was able to change so much every year and still be effective—and then give it all up to pursue his calling. Many years later, Natalya made the same change from secure paycheck to establishing her own business.

**All personal growth begins with a mental
picture of what is possible.**

At the time of Carl's transition, Carol S. Dweck's book *Mindset the New Psychology of Success* had not been written. Had it been available, he might have recognized that his former colleague had a "fixed mindset," and he had a "growth mindset." That's why his former colleague couldn't understand his decision to forge a path to business ownership. Natalya has had the same discussions with her contemporaries.

The distinctions Dweck notes between fixed and growth mindsets illustrate how we might deal with obstacles and frustrations during our success journeys. Dweck's research suggests these two basic belief systems or mindsets—fixed and growth—influence how people respond to obstacles, setbacks, and failure when pursuing goals.

In general, individuals with a fixed mindset tend to believe that their basic qualities like intelligence or talent are fixed and can't be changed or improved. When faced with difficulties or obstacles, individuals with a fixed mindset are likely to get discouraged and give up on their goal.

Individuals with a growth mindset adhere to the belief that their abilities can be developed through dedication and hard work. This perspective fuels a love of learning and intentional dedication that increases the probability of successful outcomes. When faced with difficulties or obstacles, individuals with a growth mindset tend to accept the struggle, gain insight from the obstacle, and keep plugging away at their goal.

In short, they persevere. As Dweck states, "In the growth mindset, it's inconceivable to want something badly, to think you have a chance to achieve it, then do nothing about it."

It is self-limiting beliefs that stop your progress, not the obstacles you face.

When you attempt to start a new endeavor, achieve a stretch goal, or reach a new level of personal development, you are almost guaranteed to meet obstacles or road blocks. How you think about these obstacles and how you frame the potential struggle in your mind is significant.

In the fixed mindset, a person may think that they are just not good enough to overcome the obstacle. Perhaps they have been poisoning their mind with negative self-talk all of their life. How often have you heard someone say: "I have no talent in that area," or "I never was good at math," or "I am not very organized."

It's important to recognize our limitations and to identify areas where we might need improvement. However, the problem with the fixed mindset is the belief that talents and abilities are predetermined, fixed, and unchangeable. The fixed mindset weakens motivation to excel and persevere.

Individuals with a fixed mindset interpret obstacles and failure as reasons to quit. They operate with the implicit belief that they were not endowed with the right skill sets and so think they can do nothing about their situation. Such a belief is limiting, self-defeating, and wrong. For the fixed mindset individual, however, this belief may be comforting, providing a strange sense of security.

The growth mindset, on the other hand, can strengthen your motivation and your level of perseverance. Individuals with a growth mindset view challenges, difficulties, obstacles, and even failure as events that hard work and dedication can overcome. They believe these setbacks provide them with the opportunity for a comeback. They view setbacks as encouragement to keep growing and achieving—not as reasons to give up. They believe that continuing to move forward, regardless of the difficulties, is the right way for them.

It can be helpful to measure how much perseverance

you have and that you show when times get tough. Use these questions to help you through this process

1. Do you think you have a fixed or growth mindset?

2. What percentage of the time do you feel you persevere when things get difficult?

3. What skills or traits do you have that can help you persevere?

4. How would it change your life if you showed more perseverance?

5. Who is a good role model in your life for showing perseverance?

> **Are you focused on the beliefs that *enable* success or *prevent* it?**

Maintaining a Rock-Solid Belief System

"One life is all we have, and we live it as we believe in living it."
- St. Joan of Arc

Your belief system doesn't simply influence your future; it determines it. So, how strong is your belief system?

• Is your worldview one of abundance or scarcity?

• Do you believe happiness is a choice you can make?

• How deeply do you believe in yourself, in your goals, and in your abilities to grow?

Maintaining a rock-solid belief system is the key to achieving the dreams and goals you have for your future. If you passionately believe that the future you have conceived is attainable, it is. You control the ideas, fears, and opportunities that enter your mind. ***How*** *you think is as important as* ***what*** *you think.*

On the road to your future, stay focused on the beliefs that enable success.

Chapter Three

Optimizing Perseverance

"Perseverance is failing 19 times and succeeding the 20th"

– Julie Andrews,
Singer, Actress, Author

Would you benefit from some tips on how to optimize perseverance? Maybe you are searching for some specific steps that will trigger your thinking and help you develop the grit to push through those obstacles and reach your goal. Before we get to those steps, here are some points to ponder. They may seem harsh, but they are facts.

1. Staying the course—persevering—is a key ingredient for the successful completion of your success journey.

You must sincerely believe in the power of perseverance.

2. When you attempt to achieve something, you can be guaranteed that you will encounter obstacles, setbacks, roadblocks, and failures. There is no easy path to success.

3. When you create big goals, the problems you will face become big too.

4. As you continue along your success journey, you will experience a degree of success followed by a new difficulty followed by a degree of success. This cycle repeats throughout your journey. It is how you learn from your experiences and how you learn to overcome and grow.

Building the strength and proper mindset to stay the course, regardless of the obstacles faced, will depend upon how well you have fed your desire to persevere. Here are some questions for you to ponder:

Are you in love with what you are pursuing?

How truly interested are you in the goal you are pursuing? Is it something you would like to achieve? Want to achieve? Strongly desire to achieve? Be honest. The stronger your level of interest in the matter, the greater your commitment to perseverance. A tepid interest and a burning desire will translate to a different readout on the perseverance scale. A goal that motivates you and energizes you will "light you up." That internal flame will ignite your level of perseverance.

How do you view setbacks and disappointments?

In many of life's situations, the winner is not always the fastest or the strongest, but rather the person who, despite obstacles and frustrations, still believes they can win.

This mental toughness allows a person to sustain their ability to persevere.

How, you might ask, is this done? Embracing the right viewpoint or perspective is part of the answer. Before the journey begins, mentally tough individuals accept the fact that they will be faced with obstacles and they develop a set of responses—usually positive in nature—to deal with them. For instance, athletes know that they might be sidelined with an unwanted injury.

If injured, will they resort to moaning and groaning throughout their recovery, or will they use their time to learn something new or improve in another aspect of their game? A champion athlete will do the latter, because they are prepared. When they encounter a difficult situation, the athlete has a prepared response. They know their plan B, and they immediately implement it.

Do you have a cheerleader on your side?

Most of us tend to perform better if given encouragement. It is important that you surround yourself with positive people who help feed your strengths and sense of perseverance. You probably won't benefit from having someone tell you that you missed your goal. You already know that. You probably will benefit from having someone tell you that you can still reach your goal. And you already know that as well.

Avoid negative individuals at all cost. Their negative thoughts and criticisms will not be helpful. What you will need are positive thoughts and encouragement. Find yourself a cheerleader, and consider being a cheerleader for others.

As you begin to optimize your perseverance, consider these additional questions:

1. Do you believe that you are worthy of achieving the goals you want to pursue?

2. When have you shown **G.R.I.T.**?

    Gumption (fortitude, determination),

    Resilience (inner strength, tenacity),

    Intentionality (deliberate, on purpose), and

    Tenacity (the quality of being determined)?

3. When approaching challenging activities or tasks, what type of positive self-talk have you found useful to reinforce your belief that failure is not an option?

4. What changes could you make in your life that would help you optimize your perseverance?

> **What would you attempt if you had limitless perseverance?**

Obstacles

"The greater the obstacle, the more glory in overcoming it."
- Moliere,
French Playwrite, Actor, Poet

Obstacles are seen as barriers hindering or preventing us from reaching our goals. Some obstacles are material (e.g. lack of money, lack of time, lack of help, or lack of skills) other obstacles are mental (e.g. lack of desire, lack of opportunity, lack of action, or lack of purpose).

Identifying and classifying the obstacles we face is the first step to overcoming them. Here, our perspective plays a role. Do we believe we are the captain of our ship - the master of our fate? Or do we believe we are at the mercy of uncontrollable external forces?

Do you believe you, and you alone, have been given the right to make this choice? How will you choose?

Conclusion

"Everything I have achieved has come from perseverance."

— Reshma Saujani,
Founder of Girls Who Code

Perseverance is the root of so much of our success. And much of that success we want to achieve in life requires a change of some type. Yet, change can be jarring, and sometimes we naturally avoid it. Times of change can also provide us with a good test of our ability to persevere. Reflecting on past events that required perseverance can be the first step in truly maximizing our perseverance.

It's important that we take measure of how much

perseverance we show when things get difficult. One way to measure our perseverance is to consider if you have a fixed mindset or a growth mindset. A growth mindset is usually more conducive to perseverance because of the likelihood that you won't give up so easily. Taking stock of our perseverance can ensure that we're fully prepared when the next situation arises.

It's important that we also consider optimizing our perseverance. We can do this by being realistic about situations and our inability to completely eliminate obstacles. We can also focus on what we're most passionate about, preparing ahead of time about our reactions to difficulty, and maintaining a positive environment. The power of perseverance is that it can be the differentiator between the person that *almost* attains their goal, and the one who actually does.

> It is only when you are willing to persevere past your limits, through your fears, and despite your setbacks that you will be able to become the truest, fullest, and greatest version of yourself.

One Final Thought . . .

It's Progress, Not Perfection

"Without continual growth and progress, such words as improvement, achievement, and success have no meaning."
- Benjamin Franklin,
American Inventor, Author, Diplomat

Life-long learning is required to successfully travel your Greatness Journey. At various stages of the journey, we each will need to gain more insights and enhance our skill sets to keep from becoming stagnant.

Sometimes in our quest for mastery of our profession a tendency toward perfection creeps in. We not only want to do things right, we also want others to do them correctly.

Some people are great at spotting the mistakes and failings of others. Perhaps they see in others traits that they don't admire in themselves. Perhaps they have an overriding need to control others and situations.

Have you noticed that people who strive to be perfect—to do things right all the time—often exhibit traits of anger and frustration?

Progress, not perfection, is the key to successful travel on your Greatness Journey. Finding a balance between what you are doing and how you go about doing it is key.

The Power of Perseverance

About the Authors

Natalya H. Bah helps individuals and organizations alike define and achieve their goals. With services such as team building, executive coaching, and in-person and online training, she caters to a wide variety of interests and needs. The clients of Natalya H. Bah Consulting come from many fields ranging from legal, financial services, and real estate, to government and non-profit.

As a certified Birkman Method© consultant, Natalya utilizes the highly effective self-assessment program, along with other activities and exercises, to foster team building and strengthening in her clients. Past sessions have specifically focused on increasing effective communication, preparing for organizational change, increasing employee engagement, and understanding and meeting motivational drivers.

For her executive coaching services, Natalya created the Define and Achieve Your Goals Process™, which includes companion workbooks and online courses such as "Getting Goal Ready." This process is available for both individuals and groups.

In addition to the courses she offers online, Natalya creates and delivers in-person training on project management and leadership. She has used her training services to help organizations develop leaders, improve their project success rate, and meet their strategic goals.

Natalya has spoken at a variety of conferences and symposiums. With a relaxed, interactive facilitation style, she speaks to groups of all sizes on a wide range of topics including goal-setting and achievement, project management, self-assessments, employee engagement, and change management.

Having received her Master of Science degree in Project Management from George Washington University's School of Business, Natalya is also a certified Project Management Professional (PMP). She lives in Bethesda, Maryland, with her husband, Mahmoud, and their three children.

Carl F. Hicks, Jr., consults with successful senior executives and business owners who want more. More personal and professional growth. More productivity and profitability. More meaning and happiness. More quality thinking time.

As President/CEO of The Growth Group, LLC, Carl works with some of America's best-managed companies helping them to identify and develop their top managerial talent, strengthen their work teams, and optimize their organization's performance.

Through his conversational-coaching approach, Carl keeps clients actively engaged and focused on critical strategic initiatives, growth, and profitability - while maintaining a balance between their Life Style Goals, their Livelihood Goals, and their Quarterly Strategic Initiatives.

Clients range from emerging entrepreneurs to Fortune 100 firms. His results-oriented approach to management combines a formal education—Ph.D. in Business Administration and MBA from The University of Arkansas and B.S. in Management with Distinction from Mississippi State University — with more than thirty years of practical consulting experience.

Carl is on the Board of Directors of Lifetime Financial Growth, LLC, and has been recognized by Birkman International as a Birkman Master Certified Professional, a designation earned by only 5% of their consultants worldwide.

Carl and his wife, Carolyn, have a daughter, Natalya, and son-in-law, Mahmoud, who have blessed them with three wonderful grandchildren. Carl and Carolyn share their homes in Chevy Chase, Maryland, and Hilton Head Island, South Carolina, with Coco, their beloved Maltese.

Also Available by Natalya H. Bah and Carl F. Hicks, Jr.

The Power of Perspective

By

Carl F. Hicks, Jr.

and

Natalya H. Bah

Are you living the life you want to live? A life of purpose? Of meaning? Are you on your way to reaching the level of success you believe you're capable of? If not, it's time to harness the Power of Perspective.

Available now at Amazon.com

The Power of Purpose

By

Carl F. Hicks, Jr.

and

Natalya H. Bah

Discovering your purpose is in life is like finding the missing piece of a puzzle: all the other pieces make sense, and the meaning becomes clear. Have you harnessed the Power of Purpose?

Available now at Amazon.com

The Power of Passion

By

Carl F. Hicks, Jr.

and

Natalya H. Bah

Talent and drive are only part of the force behind achievement. The rest is passion. If you're ready to reach your next level of success, it's time to harness the Power of Passion.

Available now at Amazon.com

The Power of Preparation

By

Natalya H. Bah

and

Carl F. Hicks, Jr.

If you want to win like a champion, you must prepare like a champion. Have you harnessed the Power of Preparation?

Available now at Amazon.com

The Power of Positivity

By
Natalya H. Bah
and
Carl F. Hicks, Jr.

Positive thinking is the key to achieving the goals and dreams you have for your future. Have you harnessed the Power of Positivity?

Available now at Amazon.com

Available by Carl F. Hicks, Jr.

My Growth Journal

By

Carl F. Hicks, Jr.

My Growth Journal is a compilation of inspirational quotes and challenge questions designed to encourage reflection and thought, and, most importantly . . . personal growth.

Available now at Amazon.com

The Best You

By

Carl F. Hicks, Jr.

A collection of motivational quotes by Carl to help spark a thoughtful assessment of where you are now, and inspire a vision of where you'd like to go.

Available now at Amazon.com

High Impact Ideas for Your Life

By

Carl F. Hicks, Jr.

Are you living the life you love and loving the life you live?

In this collection of thoughts and observations be inspired to rekindle your dreams, embrace your potential, and achieve what is possible in your life. Learn how to enjoy the life you were destined to live!

Available now at Amazon.com and
Barnes&Noble.com

Unlock the Growth Potential of Your Organization
By
Carl F. Hicks, Jr., Ph.D. and
Martin E. Willoughby, Jr., J.D.

With this innovative tool, learn how to understand and motivate each individual in your organization in order to achieve collective success.

Available now at Amazon.com and
Barnes&Noble.com

Are you ready for a Hicks Fix?

Visit **TheHicksFix.com** today!

Learn more about The Growth Group, LLC, awareness and growth enhancing services:

- Executive Coaching
- Team Strengthening
- Organizational Optimization

Discover valuable resources:

- Monthly High Impact Ideas and Coaching Tips
- Podcasts
- Worksheets
- Videos

Consultants to Management

Read on for excerpts from the
Power Series:

The Power of Perspective

The Power of Purpose

The Power of Passion

The Power of Preparation

The Power of Positivity

The Power of Perspective

By

Carl F. Hicks, Jr., Ph.D.
and
Natalya H. Bah, PMP, MSPM

Excerpt

The Power of Perspective

"A change in your perspective can result in a seismic shift in your life."

–Natalya H. Bah, Co-Author

Art loved the view from his second story balcony. From that perch, he could enjoy the daily sunsets over the Pacific Ocean. He found the fading colors invigorating. His colleague Dave, on the other hand, could never see nor appreciate the sunset from his basement apartment.

Sometimes Art and Dave would have the opportunity to work together on the same project. Both were equally skilled and talented and had graduated from top universities. Yet Art and Dave's perspectives of what was possible were as different as their views from their apartments. Art had an expanding perspective and was never deterred when issues or obstacles arose. Dave, on the other hand, had a confining perspective. Dave would get frustrated by unexpected changes and saw them as barriers, not opportunities to do things better.

Art's perspective on life tended to reflect his "balcony" view. With that perspective, Art continued to grow and develop and eventually moved into his dream job. His career advancement was enhanced by his "balcony" view.

Our perspective determines how successful we'll be in our work and life. It influences how we think and see the world and how we interact with people and react to events. Successful individuals have a perspective that tends to drive them toward successful outcomes. They tend to see opportunities in problems. They look on the bright side of things and visualize results.

As you read this book, we invite you to examine and reflect upon your perspective. When was the last time that you really considered what your perspective was, and how it might be affecting your life? How does your perspective affect how you see and react to situations in your life and career? How in control of your perspective are you?

Perspective is a powerful word. It's defined by Merriam Webster as providing "the ability to understand what is important and what isn't."[1] Would you benefit from the

---

1. *"Perspective." Merriam-Webster.com 2018.https://www.Merriam-Webster.com (7 March 2018)*

opportunity to consider what is important in your life, and how you can harness this powerful tool to make you more succussful?

Throughout this book, we will provide you with questions that will help you investigate and strengthen your perspective. We hope you'll allow your perspective—hopefully from the balcony and not the basement—to drive you toward personal and professional success.

A Moment of Perspective...

How is your vision?

Some people view the world through the lens of rose-colored glasses. Others see the world through "woe-shaded" glasses.

But there are some who choose to wear "vision" glasses and "see" what's not there ... but could be.

- *They see an opportunity, where others may see a problem.*
- *They see a future, where others may be stuck in the past.*
- *They envision greatness, while others experience envy or fear.*

So, how is your vision? Is it time for an eye exam?

The Power of Purpose

By

Carl F. Hicks, Jr., Ph.D.
and
Natalya H. Bah, PMP, MSPM

Excerpt

The Power of Purpose

"There are two great days in a person's life—the day we are born and the day we discover why."

–William Barclay, Author, Scholar

Knowing your *why*—your purpose—is a powerful success mindset. Typically, people can tell you what they do for a living, and how they do it, but some struggle with explaining "why" they do what they do for a living.

So, why is it important to know your "why," your purpose for doing what you do? Strong determination from the inside enhances what a person is trying to do, be, or become. A clear, internal purpose can channel your energy, provide fuel for your efforts, and keep you focused on your intentions. Once you identify your purpose, you can focus on a more intentional effort toward a goal you want to accomplish. If there's no clear purpose, you may drift off course.

Purpose transforms activity into achievement.

Purpose is defined as "the reason for which something exists or is done, made, used, etc."[1] Your reason helps you shape your vision and propels you toward your initiative or goal. When you encounter adversity, your reason helps you move forward anyway.

People who have a clear grasp of their why—and we equate that with the word "purpose"—can be truly intentional in their efforts. Your purpose comes from your values, beliefs,

---

1. *"Purpose." Learners Dictionary.com 2018.https://www.learnersdictionary.com*

passions, and what you determine is important to you. It comes from knowing that you have certain talents and from visualizing the results you desire. Once you have taken ownership of your purpose, no one can take it away from you.

With purpose, you can focus more on how you want to live your life—and maybe even how you want to be remembered—as opposed to only what you have accomplished. We all have purpose inside of us, but we have to nurture and shape it. You'll have to surface and enhance your purpose before it can give meaning to your life.

Do You Know Where You're Going?

Cat: "Where are you going?"

Alice: "Which way should I go?"

Cat: "That depends on where you are going?"

Alice: "I don't know."

Cat: "Then it doesn't matter which way you go."

-Lewis Carroll, ***Alice in Wonderland***

*In Lewis Carroll's classic **Alice in Wonderland**, Alice did not have a compelling "purpose" to propel her toward a desirable destination. She may eventually arrive "some place," but is it the "some place" she wanted to be? Or will she just fit herself into the "some place" she has reached?*

Some people have such a strong purpose that they are motivated to endure all kinds of hardships to reach their desired destination. Their strong purpose provides both a sense of direction and motivation to pursue a specific course of action. They will not settle for less.

Others have only a vague notion of what they want or where they are going. They become discouraged at the first obstacle. The lack of a definitive purpose provides little sense of direction and limited motivation. They will likely be tempted to settle for anything.

The Power of Passion

By

Carl F. Hicks, Jr., Ph.D.
and
Natalya H. Bah, PMP, MSPM

Excerpt

The Power of Passion

"Working hard for something we don't care about is called stress. Working hard for something we love is called passion."

–Simon Sinek,
Author, Motivational Speaker

Passion is a powerful force. It is the major fuel for achieving our dreams and our goals. What is your passion? When was the last time you took inventory of your passions and considered whether you are living your life pursuing them?

Passion is defined as a "strong liking or desire for or a devotion to some activity, object, or concept."[1] The more passionate we are about something, the more likely that we

---

1. "Passion." Merriam-Webster.com 2018. https://www.Merriam-Webster.com (7 March 2018)

will be successful at it. Think about people you've known who have been very passionate about their work. Doesn't it seem like those are the ones who receive the greatest notice and accolades? They live their devotion and are rewarded for it.

Sometimes we get stuck at a place in our life's journey, and we need help in getting unstuck. It may be helpful to refine, clarify, and crystalize what we are truly passionate about. We cannot overemphasize the power of passion as a propellant to helping us fulfill our dreams.

This book will walk you through rediscovering your passion by providing questions to help you think deeply about your passions. We'll then clarify your passions by revisiting activities you greatly enjoyed as a child and how to use other factors to more deeply understand your passions.

Finally, we'll discuss why pursuing your passion is

important to becoming the "you" you were meant to be.

> **Do I make decisions in my life without considering my passions?**

The Power of Preparation

By

Natalya H. Bah, PMP, MSPM
and
Carl F. Hicks, Jr., Ph.D.

Excerpt

The Power of Preparation

"There are other players who were more talented, but there is no one who could out-prepare me."

–Peyton Manning,
Two-Time Super Bowl Champion,
Five-Time National Football League Most Valuable Player

Semper Paratus – United States Coast Guard Motto

Continuous preparation is a hallmark of champions, and a strong perspective can be enhanced by intentional, purposeful, determined, definitive, and disciplined preparation. Being fully prepared occurs one step at a time, and preparation can be conceptualized as the build-up of useful skill sets over time.

Each of us needs to ask ourselves, "What skills do I need to ensure success?" and "What do I need to know how to do exceedingly well to be *Semper Paratus*—always ready?"

Intentional and purposeful preparation suggests that one devote considerable thought to the *why* and *what* of the planned preparation. Are you wanting to improve an already established skill? Do you want to strengthen a skill that has the potential for further development? The most likely response will be a "yes" to both questions.

Peyton Manning spent countless hours reviewing game film, notes by scouts, and his own thoughts in preparation for each game. He once said that he may not have been the most skilled player on the field, but he was the most prepared. A blog post by Sport Psychology Quotes (July 21, 2011) quoted Manning describing his consistent preparation:

> "In the NFL game today, there are a lot of better athletes than I am, and quarterbacks these days are faster than the quarterbacks have always been,

they're running like crazy. But I kind of stick to my roots of the disciplined quarterback. You know, I'm doing the same routine every week, studying tapes and working hard, getting ready to play and making good decisions on Sunday."

The thoroughness of Manning's preparation manifested itself in wins, MVP awards, and a number of other individual and team NFL records. In his final game as a professional football player, his team won the 2016 Super Bowl. Peyton credited his intense preparation as a contributing factor to his confidence.

Dr. Denton Cooley, the noted heart surgeon, completed the first successful heart transplant in the United States and performed more than 120,000 open heart operations during his career. He had great manual dexterity and surgical efficiency. Other surgeons commented on his lightning speed, the huge volume of daily surgeries, and his "Tiffany-level" quality. Surgeons came to Houston from all over the world to observe his procedures.

Dr. Christian Barnard said, "It was the most beautiful surgery I had ever seen. No one could equal it. Dr. Cooley's skill was matched by his grace and kindness."

His surgical procedures were focused, decisive, efficient, and effective—all outcomes of his intentional and purposeful preparation. One example of his purposeful practice involved tying knots inside of a small box as preparation for efficiently tying off surgical sutures in the confined space of a patient's chest cavity.

Champions such as Peyton Manning and Dr. Denton Cooley were able to reach the highest levels of achievement in their respective fields through dedication, hard work, and purposeful preparation. They were fortunate to have been in a calling where what they loved to do and what they did well came together.

Some may say that they were lucky. Luck may play a role, but their success did not happen by chance. Their 'luck' was the result of their preparation meeting with opportunities presented to them. "Luck is what happens when preparation meets opportunity," claimed Seneca.

The question of what to prepare for finds its response in the clarity of one's perspective. Preparation is enhanced by the clarity of your perspective. As you gain clarity about how you see the world, what you want from it, and what you are willing to do to get what you want, the preparation necessary becomes clear.

The Power of Positivity

By

Natalya H. Bah, PMP, MSPM
and
Carl F. Hicks, Jr., Ph.D.

Excerpt

The Power of Positivity

*"Whether you think you can, or you think you can't—
you're right."*

–Henry Ford,
Founder of Ford Motor Company

If you think you can change your way of living by changing your way of thinking and you take action, then we believe you can. However, if you think that you can't change your life for the better, and you don't even try, then you won't. How we see a situation or an event or respond to people's words depends upon how we think about where we are, who we are, and what we can do. In short, how we think influences our lives and actions.

"I can do this!"

Several years ago, when one of Carl's granddaughters was about six years old, he and his wife took her to a birthday party at a bowling alley. They wondered, "How are these children going to be able to lift the bowling ball and throw it down the lane?" What they found out is that the alley adds a type of bumper to prevent gutter balls for children. If the child can toss the ball or drop it, it'll roll down the alley. With the bumper, it'll continue down the lane and most likely hit some pins.

Two children, in particular, caught Carl's attention with their different approaches to the game. The first was a three-foot tall girl who weighed about 30 pounds. Each time it was her turn, she'd become excited, jump around, and say, "I can do this. I can do this. I can do this."

She'd grab a bowling ball and struggle up to the line and drop the ball. She obviously couldn't throw it, because it was too heavy. Although she could barely make it up to the line, she'd drop the ball and then start jumping and yelling, "Strike! Strike! Strike!" The ball rolled slowly, yet it would knock some pins down due to the bumpers. Carl noticed that she actually made two strikes. It was always exciting to watch her jump up and down and just yell, "Strike! Strike! Strike!" every time she bowled.

Your *attitude* trumps your *aptitude*.

In contrast, a four-foot tall boy weighing about 15-20 pounds more than the girl would complain about the weight of the ball and how hard it was to bowl. His hunched shoulders revealed his reluctance as he walked up to the line. He was bigger and had more strength than the girl, so could put a little push behind the ball before throwing it down the alley.

After he threw the ball, I noticed he would turn to his left and walk away with his head down and a dejected look on his face. He would say, "This is too difficult. The ball is too heavy, and the pins are too far away." Almost every time, as the ball would move to the left and ride down that left bumper, it would go down and hit just one or two pins. Carl never saw him get a strike.

The young girl who was bowling with a positive attitude had what we call an internal *locus of control*.

Locus is another word for location. **People who have an internal locus of control about a certain event or activity in their life believe that they can exert some impact on the result that might occur.** Her jumping up and down and yelling, "Strike! Strike! Strike!" indicated that she believed that she could do just that, and on a couple of occasions, she actually did.

> **Positive thoughts ignite possibilities.**
> **Negative thoughts limit your options.**

The opposite of internal locus of control is what's referred to as an external locus of control. This refers to a belief that one can't change an outcome no matter what actions are taken and that one's results are beyond one's control.

Our loci of control varies depending upon the situation or task. For example, the very next day the boy may have had an internal locus of control when he was in art class, and the girl may have had an external locus of control when she was on the soccer field. We're always somewhere on that continuum.

Your belief system does not simply influence your future; it determines it.

> Do you exhibit an internal or external locus of control most of the time?

www.ingramcontent.com/pod-product-compliance
Lightning Source LLC
Chambersburg PA
CBHW071408220526
45469CB00004B/1202